Earth is a planet that is rich in natural resources. From rocks and minerals to plants and animals, the variety and abundance of natural resources on Earth provide the foundation for human civilizations, both in the past and present day. Some of the natural resources are necessary for sustaining life, while others enhance our lives by providing the materials for scientific, artistic, and industrial endeavors[1]. There are several different kinds of natural resources, including renewable and non-renewable resources, as well as organic[2] and inorganic[3] resources. What are natural resources? How do we use our natural resources? What are some of the threats to these natural resources?

---

[1]Endeavors—Something that a person has tried to do.
[2]Organic—Something that is or was living.
[3]Inorganic—Something that is not living or has never been alive.

# TABLE OF CONTENTS

# EARTH AND ITS NATURAL RESOURCE

Solar System & the Universe | Fourth Grade Non Fiction Books
Children's Astronomy & Space Books

First Edition, 2020

Published in the United States by Speedy Publishing LLC, 40 E Main Street, Newark, Delaware 19711 USA.

© 2020 Baby Professor Books, an imprint of Speedy Publishing LLC

Baby Professor Books are available at special discounts when purchased in bulk for industrial and sales-promotional use. For details contact our Special Sales Team at Speedy Publishing LLC, 40 E Main Street, Newark, Delaware 19711 USA. Telephone (888) 248-4521 Fax: (210) 519-4043. www. speedybookstore.com

10 9 8 7 6 * 5 4 3 2 1

Print Edition: 9781541949348
Digital Edition: 9781541951143

See the world in pictures. Build your knowledge in style.
www.speedypublishing.com

3d illustration of earth

# WHAT ARE NATURAL RESOURCES?

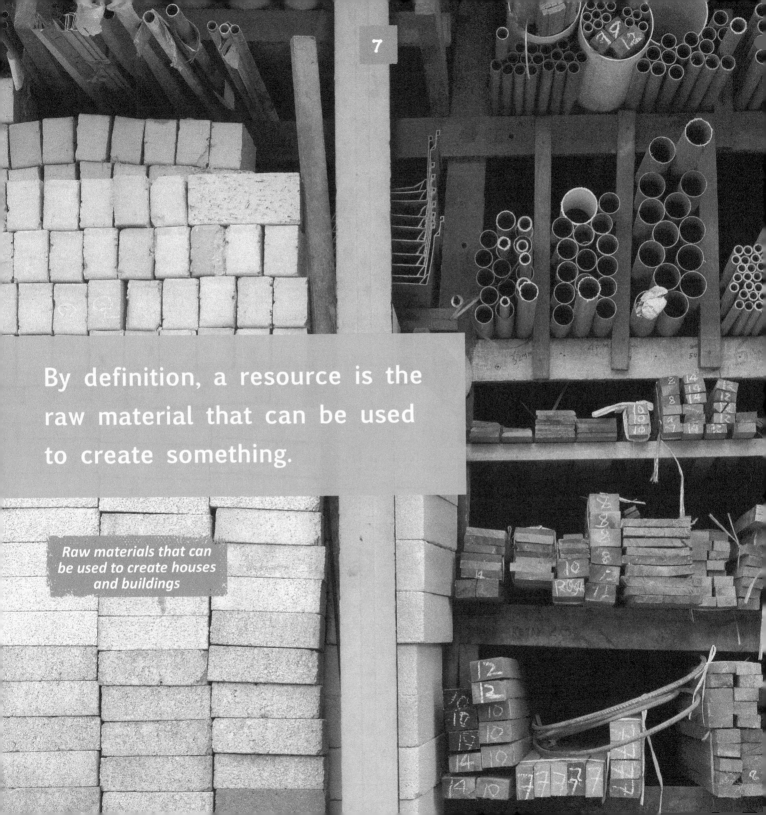

By definition, a resource is the raw material that can be used to create something.

*Raw materials that can be used to create houses and buildings*

A natural resource is a resource
that occurs without assistance
from humans or outside forces.

*Waterfalls, one of the
natural resources*

When we talk about natural resources on Earth, we include things like the air, the sunlight, and water. Animals use air to breath. Plants use sunlight to grow. And both animals and plants use water to live.

*Animals and plants use water and sunlight to live*

There are many more natural resources, as well. Things we use as fuel, such as coal, oil, and natural gas, are natural resources.

*Heaps of coal*

*Oil rig drilling platform*

*Natural Gas*

*Diamonds*

*Gold*

*Silver*

*Precious Gemstone*

So are many of the things that we place a high value on, like diamonds, gold, silver, and precious gemstones. Natural resources are made by nature and used by humans.

# NATURAL RESOURCES HELP COUNTRIES MAKE MONEY

Even though the Earth has an abundance of natural resources, they are not evenly distributed across the globe. Some countries have more natural resources than others.

*Nature's tree nursery in Tongass National Forest, Alaska*

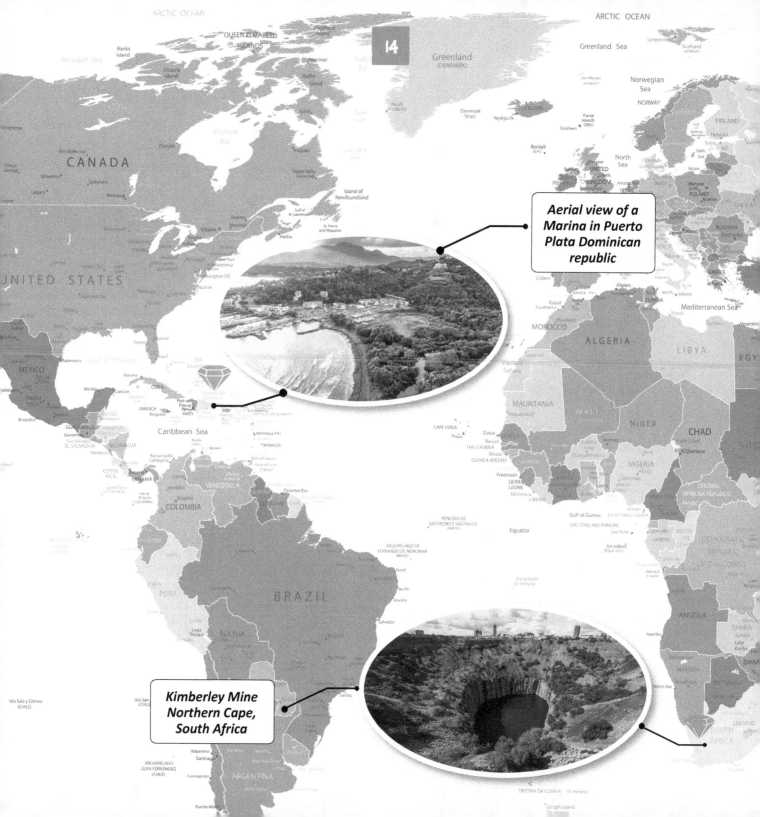

Aerial view of a Marina in Puerto Plata Dominican republic

Kimberley Mine Northern Cape, South Africa

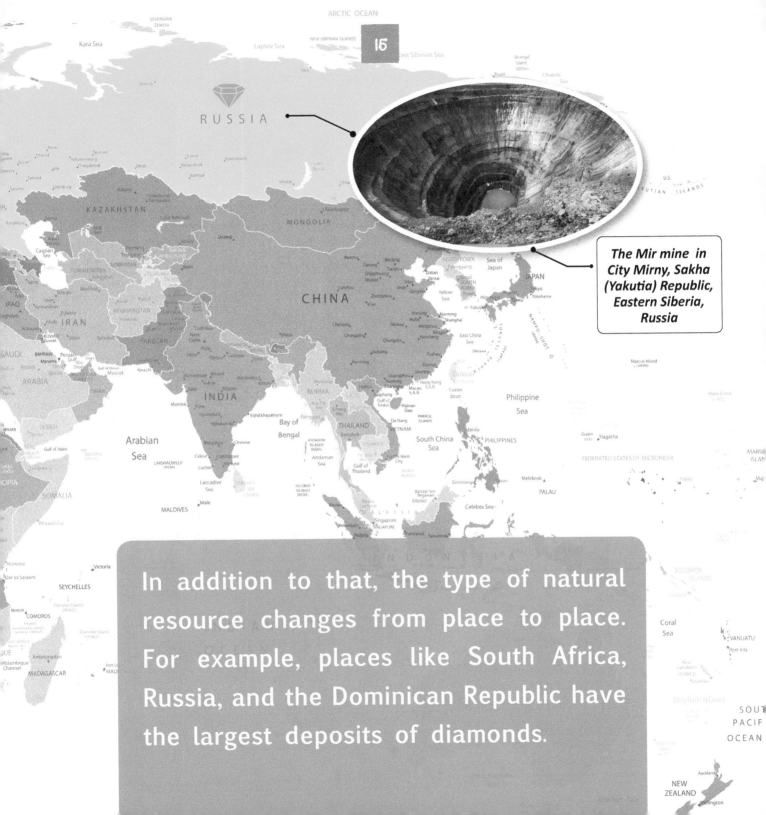

The Mir mine in City Mirny, Sakha (Yakutia) Republic, Eastern Siberia, Russia

In addition to that, the type of natural resource changes from place to place. For example, places like South Africa, Russia, and the Dominican Republic have the largest deposits of diamonds.

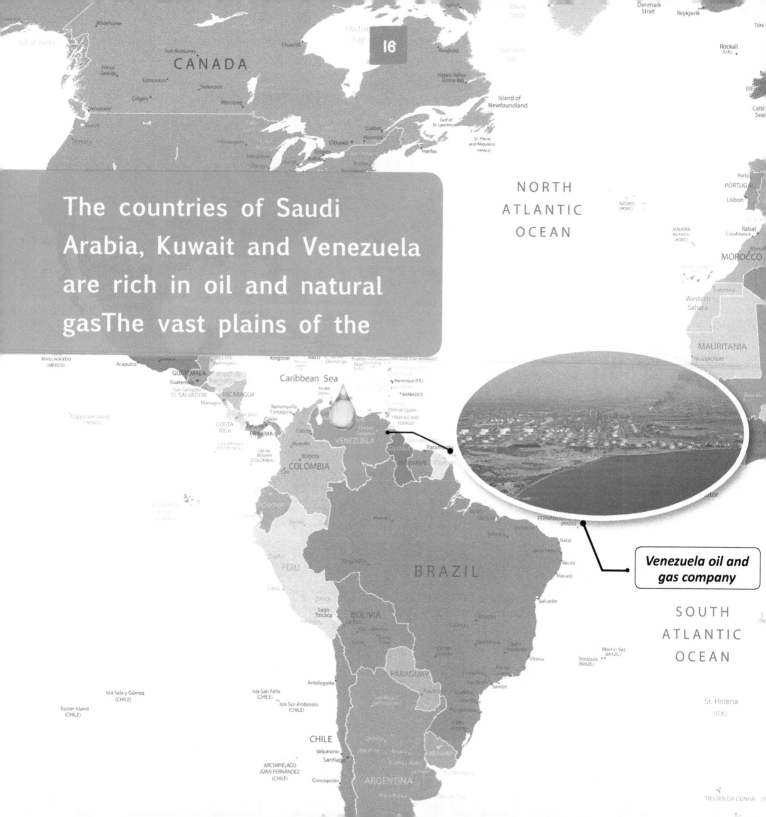

The countries of Saudi Arabia, Kuwait and Venezuela are rich in oil and natural gasThe vast plains of the

**Venezuela oil and gas company**

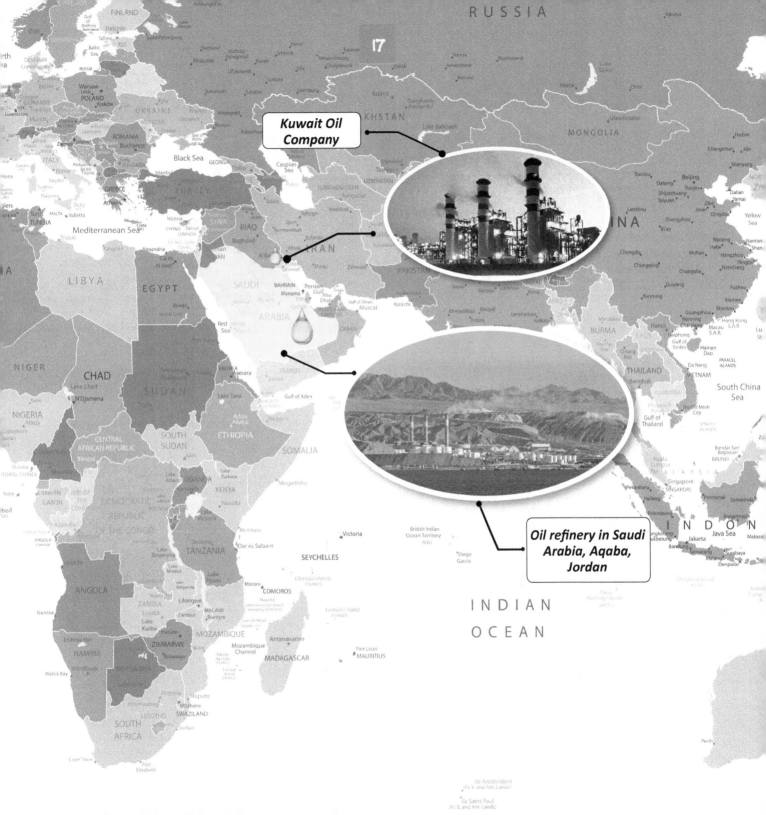

**Kuwait Oil Company**

**Oil refinery in Saudi Arabia, Aqaba, Jordan**

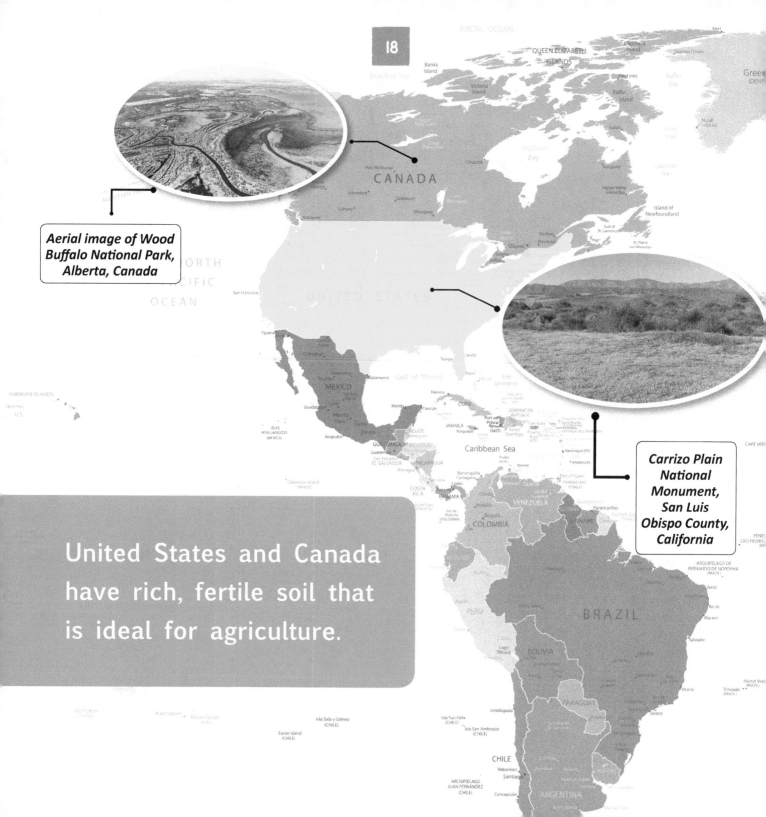

**Aerial image of Wood Buffalo National Park, Alberta, Canada**

**Carrizo Plain National Monument, San Luis Obispo County, California**

United States and Canada have rich, fertile soil that is ideal for agriculture.

Each country tries to find the best way to use the natural resources it has and sell or trade the surplus. It should be no surprise that the wealthier countries are the ones with the most natural resources and the poorer countries are the one with fewer natural resources.

Idustrial oil refinery

# HOW ARE NATURAL RESOURCES CLASSIFIED?

All of Earth's natural resources fall into different classifications. One way that scientists classify natural resources is by their origin— whether they once came from a living or non-living thing.

*This school of Blue Indian Mackerel is an example of a natural resource.*

Another system for classifying natural resources is by their stage of readiness for humans to use.

*Firewood is a renewable resource*

Lastly, natural resources are classified by whether the planet is able to produce more of it or not. In the following sections we will examine each of these classifications in more detail and provide examples of each one.

*A concept of earth and its natural resources*

# BIOTIC NATURAL RESOURCES

*An image montage of biotic resources on Earth*

A natural resource that originated from a living thing is called a biotic[4], or organic, natural resource. Biotic resources include all living things on Earth—people, plants, trees, animals, fish, and fungus, for example.

---

[4]Biotic – A material that is currently alive or came from a formerly living organism

Concept of sustainable natural resources, healthy environment and ecology.

It also included anything that was once a living thing. Most of our fossil fuels, like oil and coal, were once trees, plants, and animals.

When they died out and decayed, they went through a lengthy process that resulted in the production of coal, oil, and natural gas. Since these fossil fuels were once living organisms, they are classified as biotic natural resources, along with all of the plants and animals that are alive today.

*Trees cut down to be used for building or sold as fuel, sometimes in the form of charcoal or timber*

# ABIOTIC NATURAL RESOURCES

Granite

Marble

Quartz

Sandstone

Abiotic[5] natural resources are the opposite of biotic resources. Abiotic, or inorganic, resources did not come from living material. Rocks, like granite, marble, quartz, and sandstone are abiotic.

_____

[5]Abiotic – A material that does not come from a living or formerly living organism.

So are metals, such as iron, gold, and copper.

*Iron*

*Gold*

*Sandstone*

Scientists also classify sunlight, fresh water, the atmosphere, and air as abiotic natural resources.

*Natural energy sources - Sunlight for solar panel. Wind for wind turbines. Water for hydro-power*

You may think that things like air and sunlight have no value because they cannot get packaged up and sold, but they are valuable because they can be used as energy. Solar and wind power are both important alternative energy[6] sources.

[6]Alternative energy — A source of energy that is different from traditional fossil fuels, like coal, oil, and gas. Solar, wind, geothermal, hydroelectric, and nuclear power are all forms of alternative energy.

*Solar panels and wind turbines generating electricity*

# ACTUAL
# NATURAL
# RESOURCES

Woods being cut to be made into lumber for building

Scientists refer to the resources we are currently using as actual natural resources. These resources are easy to get to and use. For example, we can go cut down some trees today and take them to a sawmill to be made into lumber for houses.

We can catch some fish and cook them for dinner.

*Fish caught are cooked for dinner*

We can heat our homes
with solar energy from the
sunshine we see today.

*Solar panels and wind
turbines harvesting energy
from the wind and the sun*

Actual resources even include the fossil fuels that have been extracted from the Earth and used to make the gasoline we are currently putting in our cars.

Coal Fossil Fuel Power Plant

# POTENTIAL NATURAL RESOURCES

Natural resources can also be classified according to how ready they are for humans to use. A potential natural resource is a resource that we know exists and can be used at some point in the future. The resource is currently located where it has always been and, when it is needed, people will retrieve it.

Lakes can be classified as a potential natural resource

An example of a potential natural resource may be the oil that geologists have discovered deep in the ground somewhere.

A desert that might be a potential natural resource of oil for fuel production

It has not yet been drilled, pumped out, and sent to a refinery[7] for processing, but we can get it when we need to. It is called a potential natural resource because we have the potential to use it in the coming years.

[7]Refinery – A factory that takes raw oil or gas and processes it into usable fuel.

# RESERVE
# NATURAL
# RESOURCES

Some natural resources have been discovered, identified, and measured so we have a good idea how much of it is there. With other resources, scientists can only make an educated guess as to how much of the resource is present, based on information they have collected. Either way, a portion of the natural resource can be accessed and used in the future because we know where it is and how to get it.

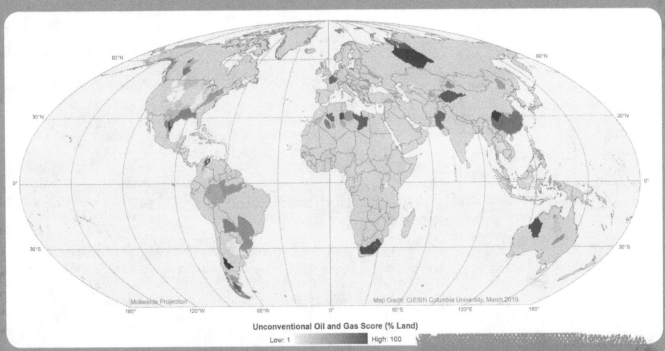

Unconventional Oil and Gas Score (% Land)

Low: 1   High: 100

*This map displays the projected future development threat of unconventional oil and gas.*

For example, we don't know exactly how many salmon are in the ocean. We can, however, look at a small section of the ocean to see how many salmon are there.

A large school of salmon

If we assume that every same-sized section of the ocean has approximately the same number of salmon, we can do some multiplication to get a rough idea of the size of the salmon population.

Salmon fish farm in Norway, Bergen

*Scoop net with the fresh pink salmon*

The salmon in the original section that we counted would be the reserve natural resource because we know they are there and we can get to them.

# STOCK

# NATURAL

# RESOURCES

A stock natural resource is a resource that has been discovered, but we currently lack the technology to use it. With so many natural resources, metals, and elements on Earth, it is logical to assume that we have not yet figured out how to use some of them to their fullest potential.

A stock natural resource is one that has been discovered but we can't use yet

One example of this is hydrogen. Scientists have discovered that the positive and negative charged ions in hydrogen can produce electricity that is clean-burning and renewable.

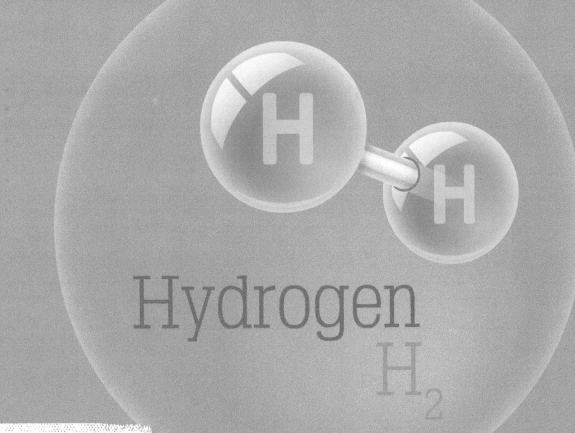

Hydrogen
$H_2$

*Chemistry model of a hydrogen molecule*

*Hydrogen fuel cell in a laboratory*

However, we currently lack the means of doing this on a large enough scale to power a city. Someday soon, perhaps, our technology will advance enough so that we can use the stock resource of hydrogen as a fuel source to produce electricity. Until that time comes, hydrogen will be considered a stock resource.

# RENEWABLE NATURAL RESOURCE

Solar panels and wind turbines are alternative electricity sources

Any natural resource that can be replenished or restored in a timely manner is a renewable natural resource. Wind and sunlight are renewable resources because, even though the winds may die down and the sun may set for the night, they will return again.

The amount of wind and sunlight that humans use have no impact on how much wind or sunlight is left. Not all renewable resources are as limitless.

*Wind and sunlight resources are limitless*

Plants, trees, animals, and people are also renewable resources. We may harvest a crop of apples, but next year, there will be another crop of apples. If we want more apples, we can plant more trees. Although we won't instantly get apples, we will in the near future.

*Apple trees*

# NON-RENEWABLE NATURAL RESOURCES

Some of our natural resources are considered to be non-renewable because they can be depleted, or used up, or because it would take a really long time – millions of years, in some cases –for them to develop naturally again.

*Large gold mine in the Kalgoorlie, Western Australian*

One factor in classifying a resource as non-renewable is that humans are using the resource at a faster rate than nature can replenish it. Precious gemstones are one example of non-renewable resources.

*Aerial panoramic view to open diamond mine in Aikhal town, Sakha Yakutia, north of Russia*

If we mine all the diamonds in the world, we would have no more to get if needed, because it takes millions of years for diamonds to form.

*Coal mining at an open pit in Russia*

The fossil fuels that we use for energy are also non-renewable natural resources. Once we use all the oil, coal, and natural gas, we won't have any more. This is why it is important for people to switch from non-renewable forms of energy to renewable forms.

# PROTECTING OUR NATURAL RESOURCES

Humans have begun to understand just how precious our natural resources are. We are taking steps to protect and preserve many of our natural resources and to regulate how others are being used.

People taking steps to protect the environment

Several counties have passed laws designed to keep the air we breathe and the water we drink clean and free of pollutants.

*A volunteer cleaning the lake shore*

# DO NOT ENTER

# WILDLIFE MANAGEMENT AREA
# FISHING PROHIBITED

*A sign on a park prohibits fishing*

Industries that use natural resources, such as logging, oil mining, farming, and fishing, must follow specific guidelines to ensure that we get the most out of the resources.

Overpopulation, urban sprawl, over-fishing and hunting, aggressive farming practices, and clear-cutting forests all threaten our natural resources. Global climate change also impacts Earth's natural resources.

An image of overpopulated city and illegal deforestation

# HOW CAN YOU PROTECT OUR NATURAL RESOURCES?

There are steps that you, as a student, can take to protect our natural resources. First, you can take care that our resources are not being wasted. That means recycle everything that you can, from paper and cardboard, to metal, glass, and plastics.

*Sorting paper waste to proper recycling bin*

You can reduce the amount of energy that you use by shutting off lights when not needed, unplugging your chargers when you are done charging your phone or computer, turning your heat down, and encouraging your parents to purchases energy-saving appliances.

Unplugging appliances and shutting off lights can reduce the amount of energy that you use

The Earth has an abundance of natural resources that we need to stay alive, but that we also use to make our lives more comfortable and enjoyable. Scientists classify our natural resources in three ways—by their origin, by their readiness for human use, and by their ability to replenish themselves. We should never take our natural resources for granted. They need to be protected and the use of them should be controlled so that the natural resources last for generations to come.

Learning about the Earth's natural resources helps us to understand just how fragile our world is. Now that you know about the different types of natural resources, you understand why it is important for every person, even young students, to do their part to protect the resources of the planet.

When you are older and have your driver's license, you should consider buying a car that uses an alternative fuel source, instead of gasoline. You may even want to become a scientist or engineer that helps to develop new energy sources that, like wind and solar power, are renewable and eco-friendly.

A man using an eco carsystem mode

# SUMMARY

Visit

BABY PROFESSOR
EDUCATION KIDS

www.BabyProfessorBooks.com

to download Free Baby Professor eBooks and view our

catalog of new and exciting Children's Books